A Conversation about Race among Poets

By

The Venue Voices

Betty Davis, Madeline Garcia, Jack Callan, Judith Stevens, C.J.Xpression, and D.D. Delaney

Compiled, Directed, and Edited

By

D.D. Delaney

Printed in the United States of America

ISBN**ISBN-13:**
978-0692643693 (WordsonStage.net)

ISBN-10:
0692643699

Contents

The Performance

Ensemble Opening Conversation
D.D.—White Man's Guilt
C.J.—The Trail of Your Tears
Maddie--Cursed
Betty—If God (Thirst)
Judith—A Short Poem on Race
D.D.—Virginia
Betty—Written on the Eve of the
      Emancipation
C.J.—Halted Construction
Maddie—The Past
D.D.—The Legacy of John C. Calhoun
Judith—Anatomy of a Racist
Betty—To Judith's Section About Prejudice
Jack—Us and Them
Judith—Me and Him
Betty—To Jack's Script
Maddie—More Than a Fist
D.D.—Bill Hill
C.J.—Psychological Warfare
Jack—Reading Your Rights

Shorts by D.D

Calls for Unity and Reconciliation........p.118

A Conversation about Race among Poets

Introduction

In late 2013 I began offering a class called Acting for Poets. I held it at The Venue on 35th in Norfolk, VA, a 45-seat theater with a popular open mic. One night a week a culturally diverse group of poets, joined by musicians, comics, and other entertainers, gathers there to read or perform their original work.

In a sense I was drafted. Several of these poets, most a good bit younger than I, asked me to teach them how to do what I do. What I do has evolved out of more than thirty years spent in theater as an actor and playwright. Simply stated, since I'm also a poet, I use my theater experience to reenact the emotional drama in my poetry.

After meeting with students weekly for most of a year, we put together a "concert of poetry" for public performance. A dozen poets participated in that show. We called ourselves "Venue Voices," and audiences enthusiastically embraced our effort, a double win—for the concept and for The Venue, which received all the proceeds to help offset major losses from a robbery several weeks before.

After the success of our poetry concert, I wanted to try another. With all the media coverage of violent, often fatal clashes between police and black youth, there were calls on all sides for "a national conversation about race." What if I offered a workshop in which poets talked back and forth in poetry to each other on the subject of race and racism? It seemed there was much to say that had not been said frankly and honestly, and besides that it was a conversation I wanted to have. If, as Shelley proclaimed, "poets are the unacknowledged legislators of the world," maybe we could say in poetry, coming from the heart, what all the talking heads and angry activists could not get across with their rhetoric. Maybe we could even find some answers. At least it was worth a try.

A lot of poets said they liked the idea, but in the end only five saw the project through to its final weeks. Six, if you count me.

They are Betty Davis, Norfolk native and retired police officer descended from slaves; Maddie Garcia, Dominican descendant of white, black, and indigenous races; Jack Callan, of pure Irish descent, who recently retired as vice president of the Poetry Society of Virginia; C.J.Xpression, a Venue-35 poet of Cherokee-Irish-Italian ancestry, and Judith Stevens, a white native of the rural South and active member of the Edgar Cayce Association for Research and Enlightenment.

My own background is in the rural North, son of liberal parents, and white as vanilla except in the summer when I lay out in the Sun, hoping to close the gap of envy I feel for brown skin.

Beginning in January, 2015, we met over a period of four months. The format was simple. With everyone assigned to write poems on any aspect of race and racism which moved them, I supplied what I hoped would be inspiration in a continuous feed of contemporary news articles and commentary on the subject, which during that period was non-stop. Every week, it seemed, there was another dramatic incident, spotlighting how raw the race issue in America continued to be, even after we elected an African-American President. Maybe especially after we elected an African-American President.

For historic material I relied heavily on historian Edward E. Baptist's eye-opening book, *The Half Has Never Been Told*, published in Sept., 2014. In this heavily researched work Baptist exposes more than most previous histories have admitted about the grim lot of American slaves, particularly in the cotton belt of the deep South. (My own poem in the show, "Virginia," is based on Baptist's research.)

The half that has never been told is how the cruel efficiency of unpaid slave labor, with its production incentives enforced by the whip, made America, North and South, rich among nations by the 1830s, only fifty years after the country's independence. She's held that position ever since.

In the process, Baptist shows, slavery also destroyed any tradition of a family structure, as parents were routinely separated from each other and from their children while white "gentlemen" slave masters fathered slave children of their own with their slave concubines.

It was a lot for our class to absorb, and for a while it seemed as if we were meandering, with fresh poems accumulating slowly. It wasn't until we'd set firm dates for the public performance of our work that the floodgates of creativity opened. At that point I was able to start organizing submissions into a script with a dramatic arc resembling a beginning, middle, and end. I wanted to hold it to about an hour, which seems to be enough poetry for an audience to absorb. The final script came in at just about that when we performed it on May 15-16, 2015, and is published in the first section of this book. It should be read as a play in which the poets are the "characters" whose lines—the poems—they wrote themselves and performed before an audience on The Venue stage.

(The May 16 performance was recorded and posted on YouTube. To view it, go to https://www.youtube.com/watch?t=107&v=17c9bh Hcxnu.)

Not every poem submitted made it into the script, though lines from some were excerpted for use in the "Opening Conversation" section of the show. The full versions of most of those poems, as well as others submitted as part of the project but not included in the script, appear in "More Poems and Prose." Also in the book is a section about The Venue on 35th, her mission, and her owners Lucy White and Patti Wray.

Our *Conversation about Race,* despite potential pitfalls, came off successfully because, in the end, it is a conversation, an informal sharing of life experiences among a diverse group of poet-friends. Some of it is angry, some ironic, some challenging and confrontational, some philosophical, even spiritual. Some is just comical and fun. But all of it tends toward an ideal of a community of equals, no matter what the color or race.

—D.D. Delaney
May, 2016

Meet the Poets

Betty Davis, a Norfolk native, is a spoken and written word poet. Her writing is influenced by such luminaries as Rumi, Rilke and Gertrude Stein. Her poems have been published in print and online publications, including *RATTLE* magazine and *A Ritual to Read Together Anthology* in tribute to William Stafford. Betty is also an immense fan of the film classics such as *All About Eve, Casablanca* and *Baby Makes Three.* More often than not she can be found standing in line at the cinema or her local video store. One of the great mysteries in her life is that she and the actress, Bette Davis, were born on the same day and the actress died on Betty's father's birthday.

Madeline Garcia (Maddie) is a wife and mother of three. Born in New York City, she had the opportunity to live the first thirteen years of her life in her parents' native Dominican Republic. Though legally "American," she found returning to the United States and claiming her nationality more of a challenge than a right. Learning a new language and surviving in "her" country felt more foreign than familiar. However, she writes, "the entire experience has given me a distinctly colorful voice...(for) navigating my roots and (expressing) who I am." She began writing poetry at fourteen in a Spanish class, but never wrote in English until she moved to Hampton Roads in 2004 and a fellow poet introduced her to the local scene. She's been writing in English ever since, performing at The Venue on 35th , among other locations, and in 2015 was featured at the famous Nuyorican Poets Café on Manhattan's Lower East Side. That same year her first poetry CD was released. *SexyNice: Pieces of My Heart* explores love, hate, children, and culture, among other important topics.

Jack Callan is a poet-carpenter from Norfolk who served as Vice-President of The Poetry Society of Virginia's Southeast Region, and also serves on the board of Old Dominion University's Friends of Master of Fine Arts Creative Writing Program. A popular poetry host at the Chrysler Museum and at Norfolk's Five Points Community Farm Market, Jack and his wife Judith Stevens present poetry workshops and classes in area high schools, libraries, museums and universities, as well as hosting "Fourth Friday," a monthly poetry salon at their home, now (in 2015) in its tenth year. The author of two books of poetry and a third on the way, Jack believes that poetry will ultimately do more to heal the world than medicine, drugs, religion, and politicians combined.

Judith Stevens has been writing poetry since the second grade. She was a winner in the first Helen Keller Foundation for Research and Education

International Memoir Competition, and her poems have been published in the former *Piedmont Library Review Magazine* and journals of The Association for Research and Enlightenment. For the past four years she has led a weekly creative writing workshop at First Colonial Inn, a senior community in Virginia Beach, VA. Coaxing poems and stories from people whose average age is 87 and who insist they are not "writers" has so far culminated in the publication of their first collection, *Chrysalis Rising*. Judith met her poet-husband Jack Callan at a poetry reading. They continue to infuse others with their love of poetry and their belief that we can bring beauty, peace and love into the world through this art form.

C.J.Xpression is the stage moniker of Jennifer Meyer, a resident of Hampton Roads. Influenced most by a short conversation with Maya Angelou during a college poetry open mic when Jennifer was 19, she took the famed scribe's words to heart: "You *are* a writer. Now write what makes people think." Unafraid to tackle any topic, Jennifer finds inspiration everywhere, especially in social and economic injustices. A three-year veteran and featured poet of local open mics, she has also performed in New York at the historic Nuyorican Poet's Cafe, Stage 72, and The Poet's Den & Gallery. Published under her given name, Jennifer's poems can be found in Volumes 27-30 of *The Poet's*

Domain by Live Wire Press and in Volume 2 of *Only the People Speak These Winds* by Guerrilla Ignition. Viewing the world from multiple angles to better understand and live in it, Jennifer encourages others to do the same—"Step out of your comfort zone."

D.D. Delaney was looking for love when he found Jala, his wife, in 1963 in Bethlehem, Pennsylvania. He's been a compulsive writer ever since. In 1979 he began writing plays and discovered a second love in theater, but she couldn't replace the first, so they agreed to remain just friends. As such, she approved his Actors Equity card in 1989. But it's not much good in Virginia, so in 2007 he came to The Venue on 35th, where he has been performing regularly ever since, most famously in his annual, one-man *Concise Dickens' Christmas Carol,* which he adapted from the original and in which he plays twenty-two characters. Since 2013, when he became The Venue's Artist-in-Residence, he has taught "Acting for Poets," a class designed to help spoken-word artists become better actors. This *Conversation About Race* was generated in one of those classes.

A Conversation about Race among Poets

ENSEMBLE—OPENING CONVERSATION

C.J.: This is a call to arms,
to my brothers and sisters of Earth,
to collectively bond together,
to see differences not as defective,
but as unique tools of strength,
to elevate character, heart, and drive
as determiners of our fate.

MADDIE: If you take a seed, plant it, with time
you will have a tree.
The trunk will grow
branch out and be...
a collection of different limbs,
each one distinct but still part of the same tree.

D.D.: If you'd ask me what it's like
to grow up white in America,
I'd say, "Oh...uh...well...you see,
I didn't know there was anything else to be.
The uncles, the aunts, the neighbors, the town,
even on TV, it was white all around me."

BETTY: How have you people who are 1/9th of the
world's population

managed to convince people of color
who represent 9/10ths of the world's population
that we are in the minority

JACK: The white man that landed here
            came with two great weapons:
The Bible and the gun.
            Their plan was to humble you with the Bible,
                        then crumble you with the gun,
and, oh Lord, they still praisin' God
                and passin' out ammunition
                        all over the world.

C.J.: There is more to everyone than meets the eye,
            certainly in my case.
I favor my Irish mother, not my Italian and
            Cherokee Father.
Dirty Injun, Indian-giver, Half Breed, and
            Reservation trash were not
names Daddy wanted us called, so on paper, I
            passed for white.
(But) was I white enough? Was I Native enough?

MADDIE: If your skin has a tint
Or a shade more than the rest
Every time you look in the mirror,
You should see a disclaimer:
"Please be advised,
May be harsh for white men to look at."

JUDITH: Intolerance—
an ugly word that curls the tongue.
In Southern forests, bodies hung—
intolerance.
Scorned for their race, both old and young,
such cruelties, injustice done;
intolerance.

JACK: This bankrupt country
      punishes those
            who stand up for themselves.
Are we wrong to defend ourselves?
      Shame on Amerika for that!

C.J.: I'm tired of that "One Day" line,
Too close to "Once Upon a Time."
"One Day" implies waiting for another
To rescue fellow Sisters and Brothers.
Too long has there been injustice.
The change needs to begin with us!

D.D.: Look through my eyes,
my ancestors all,
and see what's become
of the world you've passed on,
from the street to the suites
of police-state reprisal.

Come see through my tears,
and forgive me the years
I wasted pretending
this system is viable.

BETTY: Let no one see my grave...behold my
     death
or made to grieve on account of me
And that I not be buried in consecrated ground
and that no Negro be asked to toll the bell
And let nobody wish to see my dead body
and let no mourner walk behind me at my funeral
And no followers be planted on my grave
And no man remember me.

To this I put my name
The Mad Negro

MADDIE: "It's a black thing and you will never
     understand"—
A phrase we hang on to
When instead of unite
We want to divide,
give up, be upset, assume the other person
just doesn't understand.

C.J.: Imagine the difference made if, when
17-year old Trayvon walked in the rain,
Zimmerman asked, "Hey, need a ride home, man?"

JACK: Our gated communities and penthouses
                                            are prisons.
You think 'cause I'm white, I'm on your side.
        I ain't on nobody's side 'til I see justice.

D.D.: If I have more than you
beyond my simple needs,
doesn't Justice demand I share?

C.J.: It just takes a willingness to step out,
        celebrate other humans, and share "you"!

JACK: When you love yourself
        You don't want to hurt someone else
When you love yourself
        You treat people as equals

BETTY: I blink away the depth
At which I really need to love.
The freedom of my heart has been denied for so
        long.
That is why I could never love in an earthbound
        way.

MADDIE: If equality could remain raw, pure,
        untouched,
like a natural resource,
It would be the seed birthing the tree of life.

C.J.: Maybe that's what's needed—society to cease
      classifying people
in a country which pats itself on the back for being
      a melting pot.

MADDIE: The time will come we will be so mixed
there will be no need to check ourselves into a box.

JACK: The last poets line up
              to save Amerika
It's not about black and white.
      It's the story,
  and we've got to tell it right

C.J.: Mental bombs explode,
clearing away gray matter
for thought construction;
laying foundations
of revelations
on real estate zoned
for evolution.

     End Opening Conversation

WHITE MAN'S GUILT
by D.D.

For a white man to say
"Let's forget about race"
is the easiest thing to do.
It may actually be cowardly, too.
Not that race or color discrimination
is solely a white man's preoccupation,
but he's globally guilty,
and that's something new,
and it's convenient to say
let's forget about race
when you're the one slipping
out of first place.

So we whites should say
to the blacks and the browns,
to the yellows, the reds, and the blues,
we were wrong, and we know it,
and fear your great wrath
deservedly turned on your former oppressor.
But we ask for a change
in the way the world works
so the great no longer turn on the lesser.
To save our own skins?
Yes. Let's begin
by confessing the sins
of our culture.
'Til you showed us how wrong

was the path we were on,
we were blinded by hunger
for power and pleasure.

But if forgiveness is not an option,
as in the world it never was,
how much do I owe for your mercy?
If I offer my art,
can I too be a part
of emerging global diversity?
That's my fond hope,
a big part of my dream,
to actually forget about race,
even though it's convenient
for a white man to say,
when his race is being displaced.

THE TRAIL OF YOUR TEARS
by C.J.

Traces of you can be found,
in my high cheekbones and raven hair,
reflected in my cool, speckled gaze,
stored in memories below
the surface of my face,
even in the way firewater
always brings a flush to my skin.

When my pen danced on paper,
Grandmother's voice reminded of
meticulous journals you once kept,
detailing the lives of our people;
their rites, beauty, and ways,
sketches of faces and tools,
recorded tales from Council Elders.

She revealed that your pale-faced kin,
back then, decided if tainted half-blood
couldn't be cleansed or washed away
they would seek to sever all links
to dress, traditions, and habit.
The worst of their crimes
was cruelty; Baptism by fire.

My heart aches for you, Grandfather,
that they sparked arsonist flames to devour
those deeply treasured pages,
that family reveled in your agonized piercing cries
and restrained you as the embers floated skyward,
demanding hotly that you extinguish
the wild ones from mind.
They failed, gaining only a trail of your tears.
Spoken words can't be torched.
Using quiet, peaceful tactics to fight,
smoke signals from the mind were
passed to us, Attacullaculla's descendants.
Through your stories, our heritage
would never be lost, burned, or stolen.

Forever connected to the Earth
feeling its vibrations, I still hear
in the whispers of slough grass,

in the pounding rhythm of buffalo hooves,
in beating drums and ritual songs,
ancestral voices calling to me,
"This, Grand Daughter, is your legacy."

CURSED
by Maddie

I'm convinced I was cursed.
I was never treated the same as the rest.
I was hated, because my hair had curls.

The natural tan on my skin—
Too dark for some, yet too light to be next of kin
To the woman who gave birth to me.

I am convinced I was a cursed.
Because even though Daddy loved me
He had to always defend our secret—
me being his little girl.

Cursed, labeled for being a blend of both,
A master and servant in love and lust
A combination of two races...

Pride and joy in my parent's faces,
Yet shamed when others looked at us...

Cursed...for being different,
Cursed...and feeling I will never belong.

IF GOD (THIRST)
by Betty

If God created me, there must be a need
So what is my life good for?
Now this white man is pulling back the covers,
     exposing
the burden of my blackness and the Negro living in
     my head whispers,
"blasphemy" and I long for the photographs in
Langston's "sweet Flypaper of Life"
Please don't make me hate you

It is as if this New Negro is thirsty....and I feel like I
     swallowed a feather...
Stopped in the middle of this question...
We look at each other as if there is nothing left
Because the Negro never existed and I feel as if I
     write this against my will
Please don't make me hate you

But this New Negro, running towards me
Holding a black and white TV over her head like a
     dead body

Fingers curled around it like the hair that comes
        out of her head

Images... water, ruthless, falls down, over dark
        bodies and cement
Water shoots through hoses like
a beating heart tending to a trick a sinister baptism
gluing dark flesh to cement, buildings and trees,
making them both more abrasive and flexible
as firemen clear their conscience by imagining all
all of this, this hard breath, this flying of shirts,
        skirts , hats, babies and earth,
as an awakening, a Pentecostal repentant or
        ecstasy
or the Devil ...liquid hate teaching us to dance
        water-colored
What did America put inside me to make me this
        way?
Always on the verge of the discovery of myself
Who Broke America?
Please Don't Make me Hate You.

All this, this tired lonely south has worn me out,
To the point that my voice is blind and I am bent,
My ears empty and I write against my will.
Please don't make me hate you.

I have enough opium in my soul now
that I no longer need a father,

I no longer visualize my dreams
but I find myself pushing against an open door.

God I miss Langston's "Sweet Fly Paper of Life."
Please Don't Make Me Hate You.
Who Broke America?
What did you put inside me to make me feel this
        way?
Who Broke the World?
A Divine Slave

Please Don't Make Me Hate You

A SHORT POEM ON RACE
by Judith

Today, according to license plates,
        "Virginia is for lovers."
A hundred years ago, our fair state
        gave lie to that slogan.
        "First" in lynchings—
            almost 600 to our "credit"—
leading the staunchly Southern Georgia
            and lawless Texas
        in some beastly contest
that drew out the worst—not the best—from us.

    Think of it.
If we "know" of six hundred,

what about the unmarked graves,
(lives snuffed out like a fat thumb on a candle wick)
we'll never know about?

It was the law of the land.
And black folks were unfair game.

When one of us
Does that which degrades another,
All of us suffer, all are tainted.

VIRGINIA
by D.D.

With one child in her womb and a daughter in
hand,
Virginia was sold out of Natchez, Mississippi,
by her lover, the judge, a chief town man
who also owned several cotton plantations
and traded and trafficked in slaves.

It was his wife who forced him to sell her.
"I'll not have her children here!" she made clear.
His partner arranged to get rid of her,
shipping her west to the cotton frontier.

On hold in a slave pen in Houston,
before she and her daughter were sold,
she wrote a last letter to her former lover,
begging the judge to bring them back home.

"How can you sell your own children?" she cried.
"Or forget how I serviced your needs?
Surely your cruelty must exceed
any offense for my innocent deeds!
I'll work my fingers 'til they bleed!
If you won't bring us home, set us free!"

But the judge never replied to her plea,
and Virginia was sold into Texas,
leaving only her letter behind,
a judgment upon that gentleman judge,
forever shaming his name with the stain
of betraying his favorite slave mistress
and consigning their children to chains.

**WRITTEN ON THE EVE OF THE
EMANCIPATION
I A SLAVE**
by Betty

I thought there was something binding and
solemn in it, the purchase
owed him my faithfulness
until the end of my days.
So natural and easy it was done
just by merely thinking about it.

It seemed only the right thing to do.
Do you forgive me?

HALTED CONSTRUCTION
by C.J.

My first encounter with a person of another color
          was like a dream.
Her tiny braids were a crown, vibrant beads at each
          woven tip
framing her face in color, contrasting beautifully
          with ebony flesh.

Her smile seemed so much brighter than the adults
          around us.

I offered my shovel and bucket and we played
          together,
constructing our own sand palace, with seashell
          turrets.
Our fathers swooped in like invading Dragons,
each taking their child's hand and yanking us apart.

I remember our crumbled castle and her sideways
          twisted body,
as she waved goodbye with her free hand.

Sadness was defined for me that day.

CAN'T BREATHE
by Maddie

The past used to be experiences that taught us
      lessons
Not to repeat the same mistakes.
But instead of what not to do,
It seems we are just learning how to do it
      differently.

Laws are put in place to follow an order
      To protect
But they have become a shield to protect the one
      doing the killing.

Oppression used to be a matter of black and white
      social class
But now it comes down to who is holding the
      badge.

I could understand one mistake
But it is one after the next.
What are we to teach our children?

"Be careful of how you dress
And don't say a word you can't defend
Because the recipient may change the message?

"That in order to survive
Be careful and abide
To avoid persecution?

"But if you want to stay alive
Stay away from the Klan
Or get your own blue uniform!"

It has become a matter of interpretation,
Laws have become perception
And instead of taking action
People do what they think is right
Because it is their understanding of what's written.

There are no savages burning people alive
Wearing all white
Adorning trees with strange fruit.

Instead they are all dressed in blue
With gold badges and guns
And the innate right to put a halt
To this life I've been given—

Taken.... Deciding my fate,
Stealing the smile from a mother's face,
Suffocating the life out of hope--
Hope...that will never breathe again.

We are not repeating the mistakes of the past
But have found a way that leads to the same path
And to a similar outcome—

A beginning, middle, and an end,
A vicious cycle that repeats itself,
Déjà vu with a modern twist—
But hate...all over again.

THE LEGACY OF JOHN C. CALHOUN
by D.D.

"We have never dreamed
of incorporating into our Union
any but the Caucasian race."
So said John C. Calhoun in 1845—
distinguished United States Senator
from the Great (slave) State of South Carolina,
speaking for all his Dixie peers,
as a core of Yankees silently assented.
They feared the consequences of equality,
of social and political parity,
leading, inevitably, to miscegenation
and the white man's precipitous fall in prostration
before a rising dark-skinned tide,
if ever there were legal emancipation.
Or integration.

Shrewd old bigots and domestic tyrants,
they forced a Civil War that smolders still
in cities and towns up and down our land,
just for the inalienable right to hold white
as the color of supreme command.

But in white all colors are present, it's said.
We white folks are made of them all.
With a little self-knowledge we might expect
a white man to recognize in every tint
a glimpse of some part of his soul.
John C. Calhoun, proud rebel fool,
didn't get it at all.
Not at all.

ANATOMY OF A RACIST
by Judith Stevens

(Impromptu Introduction: "And you wonder how
people get like that? Take my father, for
example....")

Hardscrabble mountain town, born in 1896,
        Southern segregation shaped him.
Tender young boy startin' out. Worshipped his
        mother,
hated his violent step-father
    who returned the sentiment with
                enthusiastic abuse.

After one final beating with a shovel,
  the boy left home.
  He was all of eight years old.
Got a room in a nearby boarding house,
  went to work in a shoe factory
  at a time when children
put in ten-hour days and no one thought anything
  of it.
Sent his mother most of his wages each week,
'til she died.
  (tortured himself for not protectin' her more.)

Nursin' his growing hatred, he never returned to
  school;
          added alcohol to his mix of pain.
  Solidified his smoldering rage with
justifications.
          Always held low-paying jobs—
  (his bosses said he was a hard worker—
a decent man).
  Is it possible to have good qualities
          and still be prejudiced?

A son of the South,
        not knowing how badly its poison
infected him,
        looked for someone to blame.
All his life, heard talk of niggers,
        never thought of them as folks like him—
            they were "that   other..."

Needed someone to look down on; they fit.

Then married, had a large family,
worked multiple jobs to support five
hungry children.
Always chafed that he lived with his mother-
in-law.
His health failed.

Nights spent in the drafty house with
tuberculosis.
Kept workin' three jobs:
factory shift at night, bus driver by day,
cab driver on weekends.

Sittin' at the kitchen table,
Drinkin' to keep those black moods at
bay,
he transferred a lifetime of blame to
others
(never mind they were blameless).

Someone had to pay for his heartache.
Someone had to bear his wrath,
his inequity, his impotence.

In his ignorance,
that "someone"
was the entire Black race.

TO JUDITH ABOUT "PREJUDICE"
by Betty

Prejudice...that rides our backs...that caused a
        whole race to commit suicide
When the unwritten word is a beat...a constant beat
        that left us speechless,
the systemic humiliation, and as Mr. W.E.B. Dubois
        writes, the distain for
everything that is Black from Toussaint to the
        Devil.

For example, what need of beauty for half-women?
This thought that we are akin to monkeys,
No longer desirable, mules of the world,
was the beginning of race suicide.

So people can be prejudiced and have good
        qualities....
To me that sentence reeks of self-deception as we
        continue
To try and divide the personal and the political

"US" AND "THEM"
by Jack

The moment they don't like something
        they take to the streets,

yellin' and screamin' and carryin' on.
Pretty soon they all start smashin' things and
          lootin'.
I say, Thank God the cops are there
               to keep us safe,
layin' their lives on the line for freedom
          and justice, protectin' our homes.

Sure, some blacks get beaten,
          and clubbed around.
They shouldn't be out there, protestin' so loud.
     If they had jobs and weren't on welfare,
          they'd understand what it means
               to be a real American.

          No wonder our jails are full.
That's why I got a gun and live here.
          No one that looks like them
               is gonna' get in this place.
This is a law-abidin' community
          and everybody's white.
                         Right?

"ME" AND "HIM"
by Judith

What does *he* know?
I been married to this bigot
for too long to put up with
much more of his racist bullcrap.

Tryin' to have a meaningful conversation
with him is like tryin' to talk to a brick wall.
You just can't do it.

My husband is the product of up-tight crackers
who were raised on fear, and
who thought they had to have a gun for
        "protection."
Ask 'em what they need to protect,
And they'll say, their "stuff."

JACK: (*Interrupting*) Damn right!

I've tried to talk sense into him,
but it's like he can't hear me.
So one day soon, he's gonna' wake up
in his precious all-white community,
and I'm gonna' be long gone.

My Mama was right.
I should'a known better than to pass for white.

TO JACK: ON "US" AND "THEM"
by Betty

Part of your brain is missing.
You wake up in the middle of the night and cry out
In your bed, "Deliver me from the vision of me,"

Wishing I were dead.
You are terribly intoxicated from huffing
     17th Century liquid shit.

I don't know why I think I need you to be my friend
     forever.
So here is what you are going to do:
You will get sober
And you will lie awake at night wishing I were dead
And you will wake up in the morning
Wishing I were dead, but you're just going to get
Through it and that will keep you going on, all
     right?

You'll keep wishing I were dead
waking up wishing I were dead,
but one night you'll sleep and
one morning you will wake up wishing I were dead
     a little bit less,
And then you will stop wishing I were dead all
     together
And you'll start wishing you had a life
And then you will start living.

And that will all be because of nothing.
And then maybe you would have paid me back for
everything I have done for you: Nothing.
And you and I will owe our freedom to this
     nothing...

So if you must fight, fight with yourself.

MORE THAN A FIST
by Maddie

Why are we okay with assumptions?
Perhaps afraid of asking a simple question,
We rather allow perception to dictate first
        impressions.

Why is my skin a label?
Why must there be an explanation
Attached to your perception
In order to determine if I am a worth-knowing kind
        of person?

Why are we so afraid of the unfamiliar?
That when we can't point to what society deems as
        the norm
We feel threatened by the possibilities of what's to
        come?

All I'm asking is for you to give someone like me a
        chance,
Give me a chance to be.
Don't delete me before I make the list.
I am not asking for merits I haven't earned,
But after hundreds of years
I am more than just the descendant of slaves.

I have to admit,
We look at stereotypes and we give in...
Injecting truth into people's assumptions,
Giving them room to be...Alive,
Giving up our individuality to fit ourselves into a
         pack,
Falling prey to others beliefs
Of who we are or
Who we ought to be.

It is time to change that...
To settle the forest fires that have been burning
         from years past,
Fires that have left my ancestors with a bitter taste
         of life.
And today we have inherited their resentment like
         we did the color of our eyes.

We insist on fighting one another
Instead of creating bonds,
Damaging each other,
Not understanding that united, we are strong.

This anger, your anger, my anger, it needs more
         than a fist.
No more blood spilled over skittles
Or nightmares that won't let me breathe.
How many more need to die
Before the internal "I" starts to believe

That society doesn't need to accept me.
I must create my way in,
Show them that there is more to me than
The excess melanin accumulated in my skin.

It is time to change that,
To mark this generation with my words,
Shatter the theory
That I need to get back to where I came from
Because believe or not
This great nation was built on the shoulders
Of my ancestors hard work

So that today I can voice with pride
Who I am and where I come from.
I am an American citizen,
Born and raised in New York, a Dominican-York,
A heavy accent and a harsh tongue,
Exercising dual control of two languages
Allowing me to enjoy
My beautiful Taino heritage and put my stamp in
        this world.

It is my job
To let others coming up behind me know
Not to be afraid to be who they want to be.
If you don't have a role model
Create one and be it.

I have learned that if I accept who I am
Hate will never touch me.
It just becomes fuel for my will.

Violence doesn't need more violence.
You don't fight fire with gasoline.

This anger we're feeling,
This anger...it needs more than a fist.
It needs education, it needs conversation,
It needs a voice in you and me.

BILL HILL
by D.D.

We had one black player on our football team,
the only black kid in the school.
He anchored the left side of the line,
threw some weight, knew what he was doing,
and was popular because he played the fool,
rolled his eyes on cue,
said "Lawd a-Mercy" and "Yessuh, boss,"
just like the servants in the movies.
I liked Bill Hill, you couldn't help it,
but I never found out what lay behind
his mask as a Negro clown,
and I wondered how much he was wounded
by our laughter.

PSYCHOLOGICAL WARFARE
by C.J.

"You should think outside the box" we are told
        while held captive
in mental crates designed by the system doing the
        squawking.
Can you hear the people behind the one percent
        curtain laughing?
Listen up and peek through the slats of their
        manipulation.

Check boxes at birth indicate ethnicity, race, and
        gender:
labels assigned from the start, data cited to build
        prisons and schools.
Before even learning to roll over and sit, your
        destiny is a cube.

With a number 2 pencil in hand, standardized tests
        begin at age 9.
Were you pegged as gifted, average, or a little slow?
Results establish the future—how much time and
        money is spent
per student in schools judging intelligence by
        shaded bubble.

Conditioning. That's what's up at the doc, with their
        percentile charts
of height, weight, and development, cartons of

expectations;
government mandates, statistics used to strike
        pharmaceutical deals—
political pocket money earned as you worry about
        measuring up.

Credit and employment forms require labeling
        ourselves; a final test.
Gender? Marital status? Income? Do you rent or
        own? Criminal history?
Facts are used to classify, gauge our worth,
        eligibility, and promise,
to generalize on public polls and pen us in as a
        demographic.

Encouraged to color, drive, and ultimately to
        remain inside the lines,
we are brainwashed into identifying with four walls
        and four corners.
Though labels and containers are for canned goods
        and file folders,

we leap, like compliant sheep, right into their
        boxes, so controlled
that options outside the box cease to exist...until
        the system reminds us.

READIN' YOUR RIGHTS
by Jack

You have the right to remain silent.
    The police officer has the right
        to yell at you,
           point his gun,
              to kill you,
    and say he felt threatened.
You have the right to remain silent.
    He can stop you because he
        doesn't like the way you look.
    He calls it, "looking suspicious."
        If he doesn't like you
           and you look suspicious,
              he can "question you"
        with his hand on his gun.
He has the right to kill you
        'cause he stopped you.
He may have stopped you
        because he wants to kill you.
You have the right to remain silent.
           If you don't,
        he might feel threatened,
    and you know where that leads.
He can call other officers to assist
        in killing you. (Usually they
        will gang up to beat you
           before they kill you.)
If other citizens see him stop

and kill you,
they have the right to remain silent, too.
If they don't remain silent,
the police officer can feel threatened
by these citizens.
He can point his gun at them,
to kill them, too;
or he can arrest them.
Most of the time,
it's a question
of how many bullets
he has in his gun.

OH BLACK BETTY BAM-BA-LAM - THE
RAIN IN VIRGINIA IS SWEET
by Betty

After he told me that no white man
was going to do what a black woman told him to do,
I sat up like raw honey on a stick in my police
cruiser.
The words and that man sat down in me
like Steinbeck's East of Eden's warm shame,
I say warm shame because there was some comfort
in it.

He laid those words right down between us
and I was obliged to swallow them whole.
I thought it was stunning, just stunning
the way God personally came down

from heaven in this man's voice just to beat
the living day lights out of me, again.
And for the first time in my life I stopped dreaming.

When I walked into my house that evening,
my God came running towards me at
        100 miles-per-hour
and I couldn't feel my own feelings, and I started
to hear things I couldn't understand.

I closed my front door, took off my badge and gun
        belt,
walked into my bedroom, walked into my closet,
        closed
 the door and sat down in the dark among skirts
        and shoes.
I began to notice my dark elbows, my dark arms,
        and
my dark hands. My hands got all peculiar like. I
        noticed this kind
of persistence in them. They moved around and
        had
to stay in constant touch with one another.

I reached up for the skirts but couldn't reach them
        because
they were folded over hangers. Uniform pants and
        shirts brushed
against my now careless hair and seemed to stand
        on my shoulders.

So I stared at my feet, saw black glossy corframs
        and wondered
how anyone could make such a freaky thing to put
        on a woman's foot.
I stared so hard that they turned into glass slippers
        and I
found myself outside of myself waiting for me to
        save myself,
waiting to hear how it all starts.

It all starts when they put a 38 caliber pistol in my
        hand
and teach me how to kill somebody. It feels like I
        am holding
the hand of an hysterical man, the barrel moving
        this way and that.
So they put a 9mm in my hand and the coolness of
        the gun feels like jewelry,
a naked diamond in the hand. My dark finger on
        the trigger,
pull, feels like an errant slave child sliding down
her master's mahogany banister; the second pull
feels like I'm patting down Frederick Douglass'
        hair.
Bullets leave their cells like blown glass, hang in the
        air like gems,
While cartridges fall and sound like tinkling
        bracelets against the pavement.

It all starts when they give me a bullet proof vest,
a man's vest that morphs into my woman's shape,
that sometimes feels like a mistake, sometimes feels
like a father's overbearing embrace.

It all starts when they give me a police car, it is like
     crawling
inside of an easy animal that wails and waits
     honestly,
while I bundle men, women and children into the
     backseat.

It all starts when they give me nightmares that
     culminate in
secreted waters, showing me things I don't want to
     know,
like how tired people really are.

DEADLY DISTRACTION
by C.J.

Mental pictures can't be unseen,
like that horror flick from age 13.
Live images are scarier still,
observed from the window sill.

POP! POP! POP! POP! POP!
Shots from a rogue cop?
Was it a form of retaliation
in 'no-snitch' land of the G nation?

Does it really matter
when people scatter,
when the streets and our children's playgrounds
become makeshift memorial grounds?

Flowers, signs, and stuffed bears
displayed by those who care,
until the next media distractions
of those killed for minor infractions.

Soon, it's back to business as usual,
names from the news conversation casual.
"Don't get involved, just live your life."
No wonder America's mired in strife.

THE DOUBLE HOUR AND DARK GIRLS IN A POLICE UNIFORM
by Betty

War does the damnedest things to a woman,
but if you are lucky enough to be a few shades
darker than a paper bag they think of you as half
        man anyway

And you get to walk a beat at 3 o'clock
in the morning all by your lonesome,
the funny thing is though you start to feel like the
angel of cool water in cool wind walking down the

bluest streets in Norfolk, in alchemy of red, but you
being there don't sit too well with those Virginia
boys and things start to stink in your name for a
time. You walk outside and instead of your head
turning, the world starts turning round you just like
a camera in one of those horror movies. Instead of
kicking the devil's ass you find that you are
emptying city council's chamber pots.

In the academy, things promised to be apocalyptic,
God was on our side, we had the name of
righteousness tattooed on our guts signed by the
White House, a treatise of War on Drugs, we may
not have anything to live for but we damn sure
learned what to die for so that our families could
        eat.
Nothing but fragments of time, created by this
green beast feasting on our post-feminine selves
running around with broken wombs and hips.

BY BEING KIND
by Judith

By being kind,
we never lose, we always gain.
By being kind,
we magnify all that is good.
Our need to be right lessens, wanes;
we never lose, we always gain
by being kind.

TO JUDITH
by Betty

Listen, I know you pray for everything and
       everybody
But do you know when to give up?
Maybe the real question is as the author
Zadie Smith puts it...
"What are the truly beautiful things in life,
And how far will you go to get them?"

STRANGE LOOKS
by Maddie

When in an interracial setting the comfort level can
       go to a different place.
If you are comfortable you just ask questions
If not, you run a risk of making a fool out of
       yourself

Never failing,
You default into your head,
Limited and restrained,
Held back by the brakes of your own ignorance,

Forming thoughts in your brain,
Recalling pictures and words you may have heard,
And as if hit by mental diarrhea

Nonsense flows with every breath:

"Big lips, big buttocks and the nappy curls as well?
I bet you can trace your history to plantations way
        back when..."

"Your tall sibling, tell him not to take up classroom
        space
His long fingers look better holding a basketball
        than a pen....
He is not smart enough to do anything else."

"Ok...you speak Spanish you must be Mexican, or is
        it Spanish from Spain?
I can't stand your food anyway,
Tacos give me a stomach ache."

At this point I can't believe what I'm hearing.
My palms cradling my face,
The room becomes smaller and smaller,
And people are flabbergasted.

Are you really this innocent?
Or there's no grey matter in your brain?

Strange looks from all directions....
And I don't know how to feel next.

I guess I feel sorry that there are people who still
        think this way.

But I'd rather sound like an idiot asking a question
Than making an assumption and offending
        everyone else...

WHERE DO ASSUMPTIONS COME FROM?
by C.J.

"Where do assumptions come from?"
on race, ethnicity, worth, faith, sexual orientation.
"Stories, gossip, others' opinions, biases, fear and
                                    ignorance."

It runs deeper; to the personal you in this
        point-the-finger nation.

Children can blame others and are taught to love or
        hate,
but we're all adults here and are capable of asking
        questions.
Squirm a little more. Why do *you* hold and
        promote assumptions?
Do you really leave your choices in life to other's
        suggestions?

Does *fear* of the unknown imprison you in the box
        labeled 'familiar'?
You *always* follow rules? Color in the lines? *Only*
        eat vanilla ice cream?
Have you *never*, in your whole life, tried *anything*
        new?

It's time to WAKE UP from that boring, black and
      white dream!

Gain intercultural insight and knowledge by
      employing all five senses!
To enjoy a vibrant life, step outside defined lines
      and experience new
Sounds of music and accents, Tastes of cuisine,
Touch of foreign textures,
Scents of oils and perfumes, and Sights of skin
      tones different from you!

That wonder, joy, and understanding is right at
      your fingertips!
It just takes a willingness to celebrate other humans
      and share 'you'!
So many are hemmed in by fear, afraid to walk off
      the beaten path,
stuck in a world of destructive mental darkness,
      causing hate to spew.

Assumptions arrive and thrive due to fear. What
      can you do about it?
You have an undeniable choice to be made on
      a *daily* basis,
as adults, to look past what's been taught, and
      choose to embrace;
or to spread misinformation, off-color jokes, and
      hate—like a racist.

Welcome to my tough love, where it doesn't cut it to
      place blame on common quips.
Responsibility rests on you. *You choose what to
      spread* with your fingers and lips.

TRUE COLORS
by Betty

Color and Beauty are Sisters,
So to my sisters in the room, my sisters whom the
      world has imagined white,
It would help me to hear your stories...to hear times
      we hurt you
... abandoned by your own tribe for trying to help
      us....

Are you living the lives we imagine of fair trials,
      laws and rights, where men don't leave?
Is this true?
Do you suffer in isolation?
Do you understand that our beauty means nothing
      in isolation?
Will you stand on this stage and speak to us in the
      love language of Neruda's
"Body of a Woman"—white hills, white thighs...you
      look like a world, lying in surrender.

If you would stand on this stage and claim your
      beauty

My beauty will no longer be fugitive,
A new freedom, grace, a secret intimacy between us
        is finally awakened
And something sweet will fall from our
heads and into our mouths, our minds will rest
in the center of our tongues and
we will speak in a language that fulfills our capacity
        to love.

You see, most of us do not know how to look at you,
How to gaze at you,
without seeing a sort of suffused watermark of
        privilege.

Bring out the secret life that lives in you.
Talk to me about your own mind, about your own
        desires.
Remember who you are and where you come from
So that I may feel more even.
We, feeling no less than a witch in the desert,
have to find a way to give each other strength,
To live who we are,
To feel who we are,
Feel the "I Am" of our bodies

Where beauty is no longer fugitive, hidden and
        dreaming about us in isolation.
Could you ever believe in a greater dream?
Does the white race have a hold on you forever?

Do I offend you, tend to a loss of voice, free or stifle
        you?
Our eyes are windows that we look through.
You and I see in the dark.
Can't we tell each other what the world shows us?
Could you ever believe in a greater dream?

Life comes in between our legs.
Man's first acquaintance with
the world is the body of a woman,
our breasts are the first lovers of mankind.

Could you ever believe in a better dream?
And woman was the first slave of the world.

MY MOTHER WAS BLACK
by D.D.

My mother came out of the womb snow white,
but a secret lay under her skin,
and, answering a knock at the door one day,
after a few muffled words, she let in
a man she said was her cousin Jack.
We all stared in surprise because...Jack was black.

How did that happen, when she was so white,
as white as my dad, my sister, and me?
My mother, with a secret gleam in her eye,
said it was often like that in families

where the men had their way
with whomever they pleased
and the colored girls were forced
to do it for free.

SHOVEL POEM
by Jack

A shovel is needed
     to heal the earth,
to bury the bones
     of our awful deeds.
Ain't nobody innocent,
     all fall short.
So many in death
     and no prayer on leavin'.

A shovel is needed
     a place to dig,
a home on hill
     or hollow down.
Then gather the bones
     from graveyard Atlantic,
gather the bones
     from sugarcane break,
scatter the scars
     from the whip master's evil,
dig them a hole
     and lay them reverently down.

Lay them under
    the tallest of trees,
let them lie under
    the clover green field.
Give them a place
    in the land where they bled.
Show them honor, and love,
    and ancestor songs.

Put the bones right
    and let the land heal,
make us be humble
    and ready to love.
To walk hand and hand
    in the light of day,
forgiven, forgiving
    might not be enough.

A shovel is needed.

ME GRITARON NEGRA
by Victoria Santa Cruz
English Adaptation and Translation by Maddie,
* from a video posted on YouTube.*

I think I was seven
Barely seven years old

Never mind seven, I was less than five
When I heard the voices

Yelling from outside
~NEGRA~
I heard them say
~NEGRA, NEGRA, NEGRA, NEGRA, NEGRA,
    NEGRA, NEGRA!~

Am I really Negra?
I asked myself...
But what is Negra? I was too young to tell

I did notice the sadness as the word was yelled
~NEGRA~

And I felt dark
~NEGRA~

Just like they said
~NEGRA~

And I regressed
~NEGRA~

Inside of myself
~NEGRA~

And I hated my hair
And hated my full lips
And I couldn't help but feel sadness
When I looked at my skin

And I regressed
And I regressed

And as time went by
My existence was sour
My back kept hurting
From all the baggage I carried

And as time went by
I straightened my hair
Powdered my face
And still I could still hear the word, as if part of my
    name

*~NEGRA, NEGRA, NEGRA, NEGRA, NEGRA,
    NEGRA, NEGRA!~*

Until one day
As I regressed,
I took a step back
And I almost fell

*~NEGRA, NEGRA, NEGRA, NEGRA, NEGRA,
    NEGRA, NEGRA!~*

So what? I told myself
I am *NEGRA* and I am not ashamed

As of today,
I won't straighten my hair

And I will laugh
When people look and stare

The ones who are mindful
And out of "respect"
Call me a woman of color
Because the word is too hard to say...

But what color is it?
~NEGRO~

What a beautiful sound!!!
~NEGRO~

Can you hear the rhythm?
And repeat without frown...

~NEGRO, NEGRO, NEGRO, NEGRO, NEGRO,
    NEGRO, NEGRO!!~

At last, I understand
At last, no going back
At last, sure of myself
At last, hope and respect

And I thank God
For blessing me
With the beautiful black amber
Color of my skin

And I understand
That I hold the key...

~NEGRO, NEGRO, NEGRO, NEGRO, NEGRO,
NEGRO, NEGRO!!~

~BLACK~

That's me

A MARK OF SHOW
by Jack

My human condition has tried to put
        a skin on me. Some foolishness
    about its color. A mark of show,
            giving someone power over
me.   That someone, whoever they
        may be, will try to tell me
what I can and cannot say, maybe
    that I cannot read
            even this poem, and
    where I can and cannot be,
        what I can be called, or
how guilty I should feel
            for being who I am.
                        Too bad!
I don't wear that mark.
        And no one else should, either. For I
    am a child of the earth, and when

I die, my dust will blow about. My dust
          will mingle with the earth and I will
be home forever. That's about
          as free as it gets
                    and I'll take it.

SLUGGIN' IT OUT
by Judith

How long does it take to change attitudes?
America, founded some two hundred and thirty
          years ago,
is still foundering, asking these deep jagged
          questions
about racial equality, while giving lip service
to the lie, that in our country, "all are created
          equal."

"Change can come in the twinkling of an eye," says
          the song,
but the reality of change is of a grittier, more
          determined nature.
A change in consciousness is what's needed—a
          mental "facelift"
for our country and the whole planet.

Buddha may have had his moment of
          enlightenment under the

Bhodi tree, but for most of us, it will be a slower
        process—
    we g-r-o-w our way to a new consciousness.

It's the "line upon line" work in the trenches of
        daily life
where we will literally turn ourselves into that

 "new man,"—the
        "new woman" we hope to be.

We'll slug it out—not with others, but with
        ourselves,
every single day weeding out rogue thoughts and
        actions that do not represent us—
those learned and practiced responses that have
        crystallized—
through repetition—into negative habits that no
        longer serve us.
We have to attack the rote of habit vigorously
        attacked at every level.

Every day we must make a concerted effort to be a
        different kind of
person, not a prejudiced parent, a racist friend, a
        bigoted
acquaintance. We become less fearful of offending
the "feudal princes," and more secure in the
        knowledge of the truth of a poet-friend

who wrote, "Like welding, we have to bring a hard
      hot flame to bear, not later—now!"

SCREAMING INTO THE WIND
by C.J.

We are each one voice, screaming into the wind, a
      breeze of possibility.
Together we are a gust of voices, screaming
      as the wind.

Can you hear us; our currents whipping around and
      even through you?
Can you feel our hearts beating in tandem with
      yours? We all bleed the same color.

Can you smell the energy of the needed change, like
      pending thunderstorms?
Currents can shift. With enough of us,
      change can be created.

LET'S TRUST
by Betty

Let's trust and move beyond antiquity,
Move beyond the racial baldness of the politically
     charged ideal, White.
This has been a millstone around both (all) our
     necks.

Give us the joyful identity of our ancestors –
European American, Irish American,
Native American, African American
Taíno-Afro-Dominican American –
So that we all can become nice normal people
Going about our nice normal business...
let us cry out loud for happy.

About the Venue on 35th

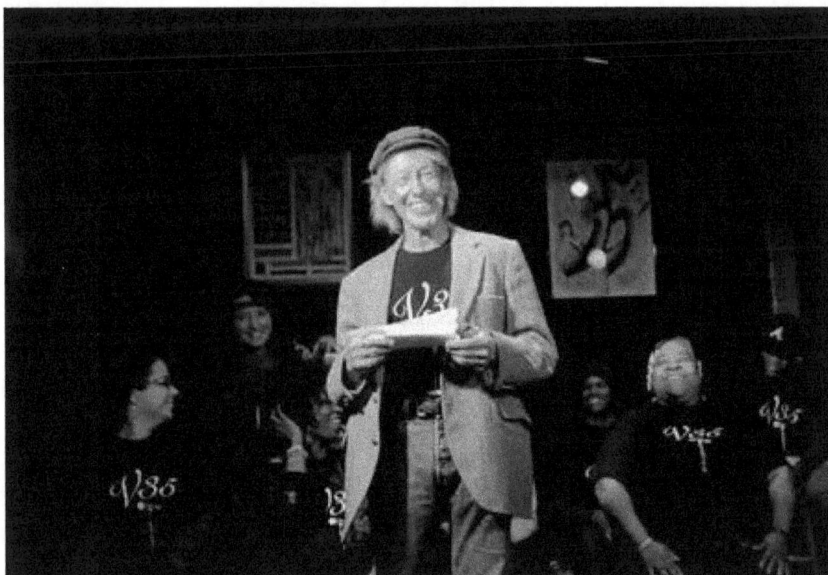

Venue Voices Director and Acting Coach D.D. Delaney enjoys a laugh with the first ensemble of poets to gather under his wing, shown here in November, 2013, at a benefit performance for The Venue after thieves broke in and stole equipment. The "Conversation about Race...." Began as just that: a conversation!

It's 6:45 and performers as well as eager audience members wait for the doors to open at the Venue on 35th Street in Norfolk, Virginia. This is an open mic night and will feature poetry, song and monologues.

*The stage is set, lights are up; chairs and tables for the
audience ready. A revered performance
space will resound with laughter, maybe tears and
definitely lots of applause! Snacks and beverages will be
served before the show and at intermission.
In 2000, co-owner Patti Wray founded the Playwrights
Forum; then, a loosely formed group of local writers who
met in a local library. The Forum continued to meet in
"borrowed space" with limited access to a stage, which is
needed for staged readings and workshop productions.
Wray and Lucy White, her investment partner, purchased
a building in 2007, and converted it into a café style
performance space, one where the Forum could have a
home and other writers and performance artists could
showcase their work. The Venue on 35th opened with a
meeting/reading of the Playwrights Forum. Then, local
poets took the stage for a Slam event. Then, in April, a one
man show was produced as a fund raiser for the Forum.
The Venue has been housing, producing and showcasing
local artists ever since.*

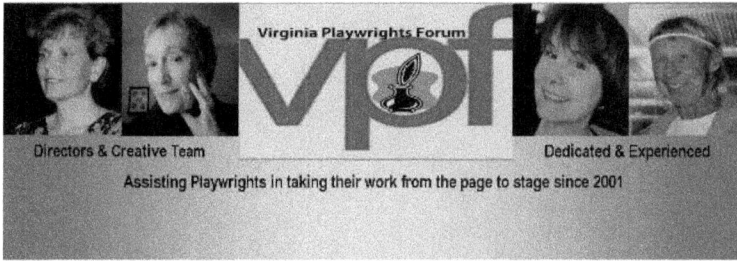

Virginia Playwrights Forum

Directors & Creative Team   Dedicated & Experienced

Assisting Playwrights in taking their work from the page to stage since 2001

For the last 16 years, Virginia Playwrights Forum, Chaired by Patti Wray and Jean Klein, has met at the Venue to facilitate new play development by providing space for meetings/readings, performed readings, and workshop productions of members' new plays.

The Venue, with its open stage is a perfect place to try new works and receive valid comments by fellow playwrights.

Member plays have been read and produced throughout Virginia and in Pennsylvania and New York!

VPF Plays were read during the 2014-2015 season at a special First Sunday reading series at the American Theatre in Hampton, Virginia. Above: (left), Eileen P. Quintin and, (right), Anna Sosa, perform in "Kim's Rage" by P.A. Wray; below: Nancy Curtis and Mark Curtis read "Best Always, Marilyn Monroe" by Kathleen McBlair

More Poems and Prose

This section contains pieces by ensemble members which were submitted to the *Conversation* but, for one reason or another, were not included in the final performance script. They are arranged in sections, as indicated, according to the nature of their content.

Overview

EXAMINING PREJUDICE
by Judith

There are certain conditions that provide a ready growing place—a perfect culture—for negative, fear-based reactions such as bigotry and prejudice. These include poverty, oppression, insecurity, and lack of education. Fear itself is a negative emotion that eventually destroys the person who allows it and can prompt a person to do otherwise unconsidered (or even unthinkable) actions. Anger adds to the culture of prejudice—especially anger over perceived injustice or unfairness.

When a person is physically or emotionally abused, it can create a wellspring of hatred for the injustice and for the person doing the abusing. However, the person being abused is often conflicted—perhaps a child who is dependent on the abuser—a wife who is not strong enough to leave the husband or partner who is mistreating her—an older person who does not have the strength to stand up to the abuser and is also dependent on that person to some degree. It is a "love-hate" relationship, ripe for bigotry to take a toe-hold and grow. An abused person often begins to feel a "victim" and despairs of ever escaping from the situation.

Are we aware that mental comparisons also can lead to prejudice? When we look at our lives and compare them to others' lives, we often come up on the short end of the stick (or so we feel), and the resentment we perceive at this "unfairness" can contribute to feelings of prejudice as we seek someone or something to blame for our treatment (or lack of proper treatment).

Smoldering resentment—sometimes a lifetime of it—can be a potent contributing factor in prejudice. Imagine if a person begins resenting another person (or race) as a child. Throughout a lifetime, that person's resentment festers and grows, made worse, often, by the fact that the person is living or working in a setting where what they are feeling cannot be voiced—just more and more "stuffing it down"—allowing it to build and grow to enormous (potentially dangerous) levels.

In the end, we have to ask ourselves, is anyone without prejudice of some kind?

If only we could isolate the signals that lead to prejudice and address them as a society, educating ourselves as individuals, and groups, at the root level. The more we can learn about our own hidden prejudices, the more we can educate ourselves as to what's happening in the larger "outside" world and better understand our responses to it.

Example: it starts with little things—as a child, you liked the crust cut off your bread. You were "prejudiced" against eating a sandwich that still had crust on it. As a child, you heard nursery rhymes that belittled other races or religions and you learned and sang them, never realizing they might inflict pain on some of the listeners. Growing up, you heard members of your family speak disparagingly about other classes, races or religions. Like a sponge, you absorbed all of this information and stored it in the recesses of your brain and in the cells of your body, often replicating, without thought, without sensitivity, without understanding.

When we honestly examine ourselves, we find we are all prejudiced against someone or something. Understanding how it comes about and what to do

to dismantle it is a beginning as we accept
responsibility for our choices.

WHAT'S IT LIKE, WHITEY?
by D.D.

"So tell me," she said quite seriously,
"what's it like to grow up white?
To be white in America.
What's that like?"

I said, "Oh...uh...well...you see,
I didn't know there was anything else to be.
Everyone was white, weren't they?
The uncles, the aunts, the neighbors, the town,
even on TV, it was white all around.

"Then sometime in the 1950s we heard
that schools in the South had to integrate,
a stunning blow to the segregated states,
and 'Negro' came into our insular world
where no Negroes were generally found.
We knew about slaves, but Abraham Lincoln
had freed all of them, as we'd learned
from our white-lady teachers in school.

This 'Negro problem' was something new,
something we paid little attention to.

"Then the Movement began, could not be ignored,
infiltrating our minds day by day,
until it became imperative to support
the righteous voices of Malcolm and King
and their struggles, though still far away.

"But when I needed to escape the war,
I managed to vanish my identity
among the anonymous poor,
where whites like myself,
having nothing to steal,
could practically disappear
behind the drawn shades of the ghetto,
where Christmas lights twinkle all year.

That's when I learned about black folks
and the shadowy life they must lead,
and I was more desperate than they in those days,
to be white in America for me was to bleed,
ashamed as I was of my war-mongering race,
and angry at the American cultural model
which prized above all the sweet smell of success
exuding from the Almighty Dollar.

"As a result, I was a penniless scholar.
Such views are as popular in the ghetto
as they are at the Chamber of Commerce,

and I made few friends I'd dare to recall
on the streets where I walked as a shadow.
And of course I was saved by the end of the war,
I slipped back into my white-majority world
but never again with the same accord,
having known the hustle, the day-to-day pain
so foreign to my class expectations
it's impossible to fully explain
to white relatives, colleagues, and employers.

"Then I moved to Norfolk, Virginia,
where black folks are everywhere,
and I was naked as vanilla pudding,
but no one seemed to care
(except, perhaps, the Mayor).
And I'm glad I've made a home here,
glad for my fall from privilege.
It's been a revealing trip for me
to expand my white way of thinking,
to experience racial equality
as a trend that's surely beginning.

"It wasn't a path I meant to choose,
to walk in a black man's urban shoes
for the formative years of my adulthood.

But it sure taught me to respect the blues,
one of the finer arts in life,
a basic foundation for later meditation
on what lies inside the skin,
where differences come to an end.
"That's what it's been like to be white," I said.

Specifically Racist

TRUTH SPEAKS: EMMETT TILL'S GREAT UNCLE, MOSS WRIGHT, UNBURDENS HIMSELF
by Judith

"Never will forget that hot summer on the
        Mississippi Delta,
August, 1955, when my niece, Mamie Till, sent her
        only son
down from Chicago to visit our fam'bly.

"We was right happy to see him—a fine, strappin'
        boy,
fourteen years old, and sweet, like his Mama.
We called him "Bobo," but his church name was
        Emmett.

"We tried to tell him BE CAREFUL: things different
        down here,

not like the big city, back home, where Blacks
could walk the streets a whole lot freer 'n we ever
    could.

"He was right friendly, Bobo was.
He'd smile at everyone, an' say 'howdy,' never knew
    a stranger.
We was worried for him; he didn't know what we
    knew.
"He weren't big, Bobo—jes' five-foot-six, 150
    pounds,
on vacation, out for adventure, an' feelin' his oats;
he were a teenager—thought he was invincible.
"But Money, Mississippi, ain't Chicago,
and they said in court when he went to Byrant's
    store
to buy candy, he whistled at Miss Bryant who run
    it.
(The Mister weren't there that day.)

"They come for him in the middle of the night—two
    white men,
Mister Bryant and his half-brother, Mister Milam—
busted down my door and dragged him from the
    bed.
I tried to stop 'em—I tried to stop 'em.
We never saw Emmett 'live ag'in.
Three days later, they found his body in the
    Tallahatchie River.

"I tole my story.
Them two white mens was arrested, but not for
        long.
His pore Mama was tore up. When Mamie saw
        Bobo,
she almost fell down. But then she got strong.
Said the funeral would be open casket so the whole
        world could
see what them mens done to her boy-chile.

"Couldn't hardly tell it was him, he was beat so bad,
        but
she dressed him in his best suit and threw back the
        coffin lid herself, lettin' the world in.
 I was so proud of her.
        We all was. But it liked to kill us.

"Nobody don't live hereabouts believed it could
        happen,
but folks from the Delta jus' shook their heads,
shrugged, an' hugged their chill'in closer.

"Well, we goes to court an' I had to 'give
        testimony'—
swear on the Bible in front of all those white
        peoples
that I was Emmett's great-uncle, Mose Wright,
        and that he was a stayin' with me on his
                visit.
I told 'de truth: when the lawyer asked me if I saw

the two men who 'abducted' Emmett,
(sum fancy word for housebreakin' and kidnappin',
    I reckons)
I stood right up and pointed to Mister Bryant and
    Mister Milam.
('Dey was sittin' together, thick as thieves, grinnin'
    like crazies)
            "Dar he!" I said.

But 'de truth took a beatin' 'dat day,
    like it been doin' all 'dese years for Black folk.
    We didn't 'spect no justice; we *knowed* 'dere
            ways.
'Dose two white mens said they never did
            nothing a'tall.
'Dat jury—all white men—got up and went
    out. We waited.
('Member, it was September 23, still hot, and
    no air condition' in dose days.
We was usin'
fans from the funeral parlor, coolin' ourselves
    an' waitin'.)

"'Bout an hour later, 'dey come back, right smart,
    all twelve of 'em,
    sipping on sodas, an' smilin' like dey was in
    on a little secret.
            'De judge asked for 'de verdict.
(You know white mens can agree on anything 'iffen
    it suits 'em.)

'Dose twelve mens said 'dat Mister Bryant and
        Mister Milam'
                didn't do nuthin'—dey didn't do nuthin'
                at all.
'Dat no-count jury agreed wid' dose two lyin' white
        mens.
                You know what happened next.
No convictions. No one ever brought to justice.
                'Dey was let go, scot-free.

"But dere's justice and 'den dere's Justice...
'Dose murdering fools told their story to some big
        ol' magazine—
                tole how they killed our boy in awful
                        detail,
                and that magazine printed it up,
                like a confession for the whole world to see.
Our brave Mamie made sure people knew the truth,
  even if 'de judge was willin' to look 'de other way.
        "'Den 'dose two white men both up and died
                of cancer.
        (Not everybody sorry to see them go.)
I know de Good Book tells us we's supposed to
        forgive,
                but I'se through with Mississippi,
        I'se through with lies an' I'se through with
                killin'.
        Now de Klu Kluxers was after me for tellin' on
                'em.

So 'de day after de trial, I gets hustled out of
town
they say, 'for my own protecshun.'
How you gonna' protect somethin'
lost for good?
I never went back to Mississippi.
'Dere's terrible and wunnerful things'
that come out o' this whole sorry business.
'De whole world is moving forward,
an' I guess I's got to go wid it."

BE AS A BLIND MAN
by C.J.

(Written in response to the verdict and aftermath of the Zimmerman/Martin murder trial, a.k.a. miscarriage of justice)

So... the verdict is out and you are mad
want to take a stand, to make a statement,
but...the stores sold all the hoodies they had.
On Facebook, your profile pic is pitch black.
Your disgust is tweeted out...to your friends.
Now...I challenge you to take a step back.
Rage is a volatile, destructive force.
Danger is spelled with A-N-G-E-R.
Refuse to be consumed by hatred's source.
Angry assumptions brought this trouble on,
overzealous views of 'us' verses 'them',
presumptions and judgment without reason.

How much is posted outrage really worth?
Change enough to buy some skittles?
Turn this into a reason for re-birth.
So I ask, what are you willing to pay?
Can you look past wrath, the inflamed red mask,
Afford serious commitment today?
It's not found on 7-11's shelf.
Smart phone media apps lack strength needed.
What's required comes from the inner self.
See people as humans first, as one race.

Cast out biases. Be as a blind man;
see similarities - eyes, nose, mouth, face!

Imagine the difference made if when,
17-year-old Trayvon walked in rain,
Zimmerman asked, "Hey, need a ride home, man?"

SELECTIVE JUSTICE FOR MICHAEL BROWN
by Judith

Those talkin' heads assembled
        to dissect our thorny problem,
but the roots go so deep
        trowels break along the way—
the problem, inequality,
                just won't go away.

Now, the Grand Jury this and the Grand Jury that,
    turns out, ain't all that grand.
Some wear the Emperor's glasses—
    can't see—won't see—
  policemen—armed and prejudiced—naked in
    their clothes.
(Is justification as dangerous as insurrection?)

The prosecutor backpedals
  takin' us back—back to South Africa,
        back to Apartheid.
        ("Not in the U.S. of A.!" we gasp.)
  Yep.   Everybody sees it; everybody knows:
        that elephant in the room is Black and Brown.

    When a group of whites gets skeered,
    sees a group of non-whites gettin bigger—
        growin' in strength, in numbers,
  askin' for their rights,   then demandin' 'em—
            they *run* skeered.
        And skeered folks fight dirty:
With force,
        laws,
            violence,
                punishment.
So *we* get   "selective justice."

Experiencing Discrimination

CHESTNUT-COLORED WOMAN
by Betty

What do you think when you see a Chestnut colored
woman walking towards you?

A breeder Woman
A failed Mammy
2 Live Crew's—let me make some money off of
      you—Hoochie Momma
A woman able to have children as easily as an
      animal
A woman who says what she thinks and doesn't do
      anything about it
because no one really cares what she thinks anyway
The best actors in the entire world...living two
      lives...one for them and one for you
A Sarah Baartman, a Hottentot Venus, a woman
      always under sexual surveillance
Public domain
A beast of burden
Hot Chocolate
A Hundred Dollar Misunderstanding
A woman who needs permission to desire
Terror and Desire
OR
One of the most interesting girls in this country
A quiet dignity and grace

A Woman
A woman who loves herself and fought like hell to
    get there

Addenda: The linking of Black women and
animals is revealed in the following description of
an African woman published in an 1878
anthropology text:

*"She has a way of pouring her lips exactly like
what we have observed in the orangutan. Her
movements had something abrupt and fanatical
about them. Remind one of those of the ape. Her
ear was like that of many apes. These are animal
characters. I have never seen a human head more
like an ape than that of this woman."*

APOLOGETIC PERSPECTIVE
by C.J.

Apologies aren't real unless felt, in the heart and
    gut.
Said *"to get you off my back and shut you up"* is
    noticeably
different from "I'm truly regretful for my words or
    actions."
Taking the blame, atoning for things you did not
    do,
lets someone *else* off the hook and rings hollow,

too.

"*I'm sorry*" from <u>my</u> lips is conditional; it must be
  meant
and for *specific* circumstance.

To those who see a source of oppression, violence,
hate, or danger in me, *because* of my pale face,
I'm sorry my fair pigmentation awakens those
  feelings.

It's terrible to be judged simply by skin tone or
  race;
mistreated, considered second class, or even killed
  due to it.
Genuine, first hand apologies are rare for centuries
  old actions,
but we all *can* work together to ensure history stops
  repeating.

There is more to everyone than meets the eye,
  certainly in my case.
I favor my Irish mother, not my Italian and
  Cherokee father.
Dirty Injun, Indian giver, Half Breed, and
  Reservation Trash were not
names Daddy wanted us called, so on paper, I
  passed for white.
Publically omitting *my truth* created internal
  conflict. Was I white *enough*?
Was I Native *enough?* Half of me blamed for

exterminating the other half.
To all those who don't fit neatly in a box, I'm sorry
     we are *still* labeled 'Other'.

Maybe that's what's needed—society to cease
     classifying people
in a country which pats itself on the back for being
     a melting pot.
Until we stop categorizing infants at birth based on
     check boxes of parents,

until we stop conditioning children to circle and
     isolate differences,

until we stop being hired, promoted, and approved
     for loans
based on melanin level, instead of personal
     strengths and merits,
I'm sorry *for America*, which will rot in turmoil,
     resembling only molding fondue.

READ THE FINE PRINT
by Maddie

We should put in a request
If your skin has a tint
Or a shade more than the rest
Every time you look in the mirror
You should see a disclaimer:

Please be advised,
May be harsh for white men to look at.
You might make them unable to relate,
Make them think they have superpower
Or give them a superiority complex.

You will be mistreated and underpaid,
Have to do the same work twice
To prove the first time right wasn't a mistake.

Will be placed in categories based on pigmentation,
Will be subject to labels and classifications.

Instead of being described by a color
They will use degrading words,
And unless you are a genius you will not be taken
      seriously.

The expectation bar will be set really low,
Your physical characteristics ridiculed.

Your progress will not be celebrated
And your failures will be expected.

Fear will be awakened
The minute your blackness is detected.

But just below the label,
Don't forget to read the fine print,

which becomes legible when your hands point to
      the sky and you are on your knees

Labels at your hands and labels at your feet
That you'll display on your back for white man to
      read:

If you can read this
Don't underestimate me
My skin color has developed into a cloak
designed to protect me.

I don't need to apologize for my color, my
features or my uniqueness.
If you have a problem, take it on with the one who
      made me—God.

Don't be surprised, I am smarter than you think
      I am.
I've had a life time of proving myself to the white
      man and to the black.

I am stronger than I appear.
Enduring many generations of physical and verbal
      punishment,
I steer from the belief
That if I can dream it, it could be,
That I am beautiful even if I don't look like you.
My vision has been expanded to beyond horizon's
      view.

You will have a choice—
Follow me to where I'm going or stay stuck.

The time will come
We will be so mixed that there will be no need to
         check ourselves into a box.
A day when
It will auto default
To human race

And if you don't believe me
Review the fine print
Starting where it reads:
Don't underestimate me...

UNDERSTAND
by Maddie

"It's a black thing and you will never understand,"
A phrase we hang on to
To create distance from the rest.

It's easier to give up,
To be upset and assume
The person at the other end of the conversation
Just doesn't understand.

Or is it you...

97

That refuses to be understood?
Let's pause and elaborate:

We are set
That the mind can only relate
By being placed in a certain space
When in reality all you have to do
Is dig deep to the root of what's felt.

Situations are ingrained in our brains
Not by what happens
But by the emotions that immortalize the particular
    event
By the feelings they awake.

As we get older, just like language
Our knowledge of emotions expands
And we learn to categorize feelings in our cortex.

We put them in shelves
And relate them to particular events.
But that's the big mistake we make.

One cannot assume "your feeling" of rejection
Is worse than the one I felt.
Because yours is black and mine is beige?
My pain is less because it's lighter?
Does that make sense?
Pain is pain and it hurts regardless of your shade.

We focus so much on what makes us different
Rather than what makes us the same.
What would be the basis of racism if our skin colors
weren't part of the game?

We are blessed and cursed by our sight.
We have given it the power to decide what goes
          where
By how similar they look, according to our eyes...
Don't be naive:
If you take a seed, plant it,
With time you will have a tree.
The trunk will grow, branch out and be...
A collection of different limbs,
Each one distinct
But still part of the same tree.

Exposure will be the key.
I can't expect you to relate to my story
If you don't hear me speak...

Will you ever fully understand what it means to be
          me?
Maybe not,
But it shouldn't be a white, black or Hispanic thing.
It should be "a you, me, an us thing."
Our past should be a marker on our path
To show where we used to be and not where
          we're at.
Don't let it keep you stagnant.

If equality could remain raw, pure, untouched,
Like a natural resource,
It would be the seed birthing the tree of life
And all of us would be different branches but
        unified....
Hang on to that before you disregard me for not
        being black.

You might be surprised how much of you is me,
How much of each other we understand.

UNTITLED
by Betty

I find it interesting that the darkest people on the
        stage
are trying to understand each other, as if that's
        possible.
It feels more like a test. You know those tests in
        school that test your ability
to understand something when it really means
        nothing,
While others stay on the periphery,
Talk like men,
Talk about their father's and politics....
It feels like I am doing all the dirty work...
Answer me this...
What do White people talk about?
How have your people who are 1/9th of the world's

population
managed to convince
people of color, who represent 9/10ths of the
     world's population
that we are the minority.

Another colonial legacy:
If you are Black, step back
If you are Brown, stick around.
If you are Yellow, you are mellow.
If you are White, you are all right...
This little ditty is known all over the World;
     this supports
a system of White Supremacy....of white genetic
     survival.
As Dr. Frances C. Welsing states, this is a
     celebration of the rape of our grandmothers

Where does the phrase Mother Fucker come from
and why do so many Black folks use it?
     This is just another phrase
born of the system supporting white genetic
     supremacy.

There are 5 categories of People:
Man
Woman
Boy
Girl
Child

The Man - often used to describe the White Man.
Black men did not want to be called boy...
      so what is left? Child.
Black men often call women Momma.
Homes are often referred to as cribs.
So that leaves child
Hence the phrase Mother Fucker....

From the Front Lines

HUFFING BLUE –LOVE
by Betty
(Inspired by "Plastic War" by Harlen Capen)

It all started when they put a 38 caliber pistol
in my hand and told me I could kill somebody,
with the first shot the barrel, moving this way and
      that,
feels like I am holding the hand of a hysterical
      man.
But the coolness of the 9mm feels like jewelry,
like a naked diamond in the hand.

My finger on the trigger... squeezing... pulling,
feels like an errant slave-child sliding down
the mahogany bannister of her blind master.

The second pulling...squeezing...less guilt now...
      feels
like the patting down of Mr. Frederick Douglass's
      hair,
bullets leave their cells like blown glass - silver
      plumes,
rubies and sapphires—cartridges spent, hit plastic
            pavement
like tinkling bracelets and I walk away from
      them...I walk away
from them like I am listening to Billy Holiday in the
      dark.

**ENCOUNTERS AT THE END OF THE
WORLD...QUEEN OF THE SWAY...WHY
DON'T YOU JUST LIVE?**
by Betty

Imagine me pacing back and forth in my mother's
      L-shaped kitchen
Trying to write the truth about this...

I've been mostly afraid in my life ....constantly
      thrown into the sun, my nerves are finished.
And loving you the way that death moves, carrying
      the force of danger in my hands and
      no matter what,

Swaying in the dark in watery moonlight, working
      with men the color of sugar.
Some had eyes like bats determined to make a fool
      of me in phases, while others,
Watching me for hours and hours and hours... are
      thrown into a long-necked suckling fit,
      twisted
by a first looking in...with their perfumed
      hermaphrodite.

If they could just lean against my breast in silence,
      it would purge this false scent of romance.

So like a clarion rose...fallen down some spiritual
      gap
I put down the nettling sun ... work in the black
      crust of day...
night... I stop walking in the open... I walk in
      alleyways.
My private sanctuary .... You may think it
      ungraceful... burlesque
but each night I took a solar walk into the light.... I
      was Queen of the Sway
...I will myself into existence out of the darkness ...

One night I see a man walking towards me, my
      alleyway on Granby Street....
He moves like a lying ghost...walks faster than he
      knows

how to walk...he is taller than the year my mother
       died...his skin so wet he looks as if
He has just stepped out of the shower....as beautiful
       as daylight....
Within 7 feet...I notice his hands...he seems to
       suppress an appetite in his hands....
I do the same as my hand rests on my gun...
       Within 3 feet...I see his eyes,
they are like shiny appliances...his breath smells of
       cold fish
and peppermint...he is in pain. I ask him if he is all
       right...his hands relax...his breath calms
I too relax. He says he is all right and we part ways.
       Within 5 minutes the dispatcher
Announces the robbery of a nearby hotel...
       describes the gunman.... Most police
       shootings occur within 7 feet.
You might think the ending indecent...but thy will
       be done...there was
Great Breath...it was magic...and it was everything
       that I wanted.

MONSTERS – ON THE OTHER SIDE OF MIDNIGHT RESUSCITATING GIRTH
by Betty

Sometime before midnight
on Thanksgiving
I responded to a call for help.

A woman was shot by her lover,
her wound was between her legs.

I found her in the snow
on the front lawn, she had to talk to
somebody and spoke to me
and held my hand, I covered her while waiting
for the ambulance and back up.

Her lover, a Brown man with green eyes,
was arrested on the other side of midnight,
the woman was what the world imaged to be White.

After my shift, my God held me down,
ran his fingers through my hair, held me like a
      Holy Book,
and spooned me into fire.

GHETTO BLUES
by D.D.

In '69, we moved back to San Francisco—
upstairs, on Pierce, near Filmore Street—
and my dog would lean on his elbow in the window
and howl in a mournful key.
"Owwuuuuu. Owwuuuuu."
The prostitutes would giggle and wave up at him.
"What's-a-mattah, baby, you lonely?
Ah-ha-ha, hee-hee-hee!"

He liked the prostitutes,
but he didn't like the city,
so he sang those old ghetto blues.

I remember, you and I, out walking one night,
the streets mostly dark and deserted,
when a large black man came strolling our way,
his hands in his leather coat pockets.
"You got a cigarette, brother?" he asked with a grin,
standing there, blocking my way.
I had no cigarettes, but I was high,
and to show my ID I looked straight in his eyes,
and after a muddy long moment crept by,
I saw two fires in a jungle clearing,
somewhere far far away, burning.
Then he laughed, shook my hand,
stood aside, let us pass,
and we knew we were part of the ghetto at last.

Later, we moved down the hill
to the place next to Deboce Park,
where a year or so before, we were told,
from a window, the two cops were shot.
My dog liked it there so much better,
took his puppies on runs round the grounds
and added to some bitches' litters.
My little man, the model for all sentient critters.

Alas, he died long ago,
shot by an unfriendly neighbor

before we were busted down on the farm.
It may have been country, but it was still ghetto.
I never really left that behind.
In my heart, in my soul,
those ghetto blues rule,
and I, too, still sing: "Owwuuuu. Owwuuuu."

Ensemble Shorts

UNIQUE
by Maddie

"Every one is different,
walking, dreaming, doing, achieving, enjoying life
    at a different pace.
We can't pretend to fit a mold that was designed for
    someone else.
When we do that, we fail to comprehend that there
    are no two alike.
There are behaviors I may want to adapt but at the
    end that is not who I want to be.
If I want my life to be meaningful I must become
    the best version of Maddie....unique!"

FIVE BY C.J.

1.
You act like you're psychic, assuming my race,

background, and intentions by looking at my face.
Isn't that the same thing you complain about
and yet you feel it's ok to take that same route?

2.
BOOM! The sun flickered and lights went out!
Think dispute over differences are gone?
Nope, now we'll debate the sound of one's shouts.

3.
Pictures A, B, C, and D on homework at age five
Directions say: Circle the one that's not the same,
Starting habits of dividing by looks all our lives.
Circle the similarities should be our new game.

4.
"Mommy, how come I can't play with them
        anymore?"
"Because they're black or white or have slanted
        eyes."
Hatred is taught by those seeking to settle scores.
Fear and anger must die for humanity to rise.

5.
"Don't talk to strangers" is a good common-sense
        rule,
safety taught to children who go to school.
"Don't connect with those different from you,"
when adult stunts growth, isolates, and makes you
        a fool.

TIRED
by C.J.

I'm tired of that 'One Day' line,
Too close to 'Once Upon a Time.'
Too long have the bad boys dressed in blue,
harassed our people, like me and you.
Too long have they given good cops a bad rap,
Citizens have had too long a civic nap.
'One Day' implies waiting for another
To rescue fellow Sisters and Brothers.
Too long has there been injustice
The change needs to begin with us!

SHORTS BY BETTY

THE DUMP—A TALK ABOUT NOTHING

Essentially we are talking about nothing,
Trying to figure out how something came out of
    nothing.
That something is a racial being born out of
    colonialism,
A way of making life predictable

BLOOD LINES

Man's first taste of blood
Is circumcision.

110

Is this to blame for this bloodlust,
This fear of genetic annihilation?

THIS ESCAPE CONVERSATION IS NOTHING BUT A GREAT ESCAPE

What if I were to tell you
That I am not interested
In your opinion about race,
That I am only interested in
The great equalizer,
Health insurance.

NAKED LEGS
(*Inspired by Harlen Capen*)

Surely, you are not a political being, but
        a deep introversion. You are like
two dark ribbons
        abandoned by the careless hair of a girl
running away from something,
a lovely curtsy on bent knees and staggering feet,
        a rose strewn into the afterlife.

SHORT

Ntozake Shange's Guardian Angel
retired after Plessey vs. Ferguson.
My Guardian Angel

will retire when the U word
comes back, Universal.

BLACK MADONNA

I know you are a sack of black cats
afraid to love me, but I dare you....
I dare you to get out
of your quiet bed, come here

to me now and love me like a Pagan.
I promise you, it will hurt.

WHEN A WOMAN WALKS

When Beauty walks inside a woman
It is revolutionary....
Her hips play with sweet feelings,
are moved by secret squalls born
on the moon and bid the hottest
crystals wild, into the air....

UNTITLED

I'd like to stand down in love's honor
and his gushes. For this is the last great sanctuary
Of my soul, my sister's soul, my mother's soul, my
        grandmother's soul.
No longer blinded or held down by the animosity of
the sun, but kissed by mere candle light that
        illumines.

UNTITLED

I walked through a gate on fire,
Covered with blooming roses,
All the time feeling,
All the time feeling
Exuberate love.

UNTITLED

I want it
I want it all the time,
The rustle, the rustle,
The tensile strength of scar tissue that
Protects my heart from fit or not fit to be
Tied. I can't bear to tell the difference.

UNTITLED

There is bitter and beauty in the world,
Men, women and children
Where sleep is fast becoming wanderlust,
Where city boundaries are necropolis and
Children light a torch in a crater of boiling
Lava to light the way of the dead.

SHORTS BY D.D.

BECAUSE

Because I'm an artist
I admire all great art,
and I admire the honest minds
who tell a truth without bias,
something we can all understand,
even if it rattles us.

UPS AND DOWNS

Poor people dream of becoming rich,
rich people forget they were ever poor
until the Wheel of Fortune turns,
raising one to replace the other
in the cosmic casino of change.
Is anyone else tired of this game?

WHO?

Jazz late at night reminds me
of Bessy Smith and Billy Holiday
and the South that brought them up
and put them back down dead.
And I wonder:
Who will receive the wrath of the racists
if ever racism is erased

from the catalogue of human hate?
Who will accept that burden?

CHUCKY SIMMS

Chucky Simms played guard for Edward Hand,
where all the black kids went to school
when I managed the rival Reynolds five,
in the callow years of junior high,
and Chucky wanted to fight with someone
after they lost our cross-town rivalry,
and wouldn't you know he picked on me,
the last one out of the locker room.
I declined the opportunity.
Awkwardly.
He grew up, eventually, to become a cop,
enforcing the white man's codes,
and investigated my bicycle robbery.
I didn't recognize him then,
and he didn't remember me.

TWO QUESTIONS

If I have more than you,
beyond my simple needs,
does Justice not compel I share?
And if there's harvest to be found
in gardens gone to seed,
doesn't Duty call me there?

INHERITED INJUSTICE

My family expected more of me,
but what they meant was security,
(and, I think, a male heir, too.)
But that to me was injustice—
to continue with that line,
taking the opportunities made ready
for those who were born to success,
while disproportionate numbers of others
are expected to settle for less.
I prefer a commonwealth of simplicity.
Please don't invent a cure for me.

WHEN THE MAJORITY IS POOR

When the majority in any country
is poor and deprived of their rights,
that's no democracy, it's tyranny,
and, as history repeatedly shows,
is sure to fall into ruins one day
under the weight of its own infamy.

A LITTLE WHISKEY

What a little whiskey will do to a man!
I felt good, so I tried to feel better,
but it only spun me around and down
'til I remembered that poisonous letter

you sent when you wouldn't say to my face
that you could never bear the social disgrace
of living with a man of my color.

JUSTICE REQUIRES....

Justice requires....balance.
Two sides of a scales weighing equally.
But when no two sides are at variance,
Justice could be the end of history.

Then what will we put into poetry,
into music, painting, and dance,
if Justice settles everything,
leaving nothing to Chance?

TEAR IT DOWN

"Tear it down! Tear it all down!"
is a desperate cry for help
from victims of a frightening world,
who only want some cause to hope.

The smart ones learn to claim a place
in a world elastic as a charm,
while others find it less opaque
to live and die and do no harm.

But the revolutionary's cry
to tear the fucking system down
is drama without resolution,
which isn't really a revolution.

CPT

In an inter-racial setting
we made the strategic mistake
of having to catch the last bus of the day
when we didn't know which way to take
to the station before we'd be too late.

"Don't y'all worry, you'll be on time.
It's not that far. We'll walk you there,"
our dark-skinned hosts assured us, grinning,
and they strolled with us down many blocks,
joking and jiving with a casual air
while we anxiously watched our clocks.

The last passenger was loading onto the bus
as we ran across the parking lot,
waving farewell to our hosts.
But I wondered if they'd purposely tried
to get us anxious and even provoked?
Or did they know something we didn't?
About time? And how to enjoy it the most?

Calls for Unity and Reconciliation

SWEET TALKER
by Betty

I try to speak to you
In a way that is respectable,
In a way that corroborates our existence
Because I know what happened was a sort
Of strange fiction.
Yet, I can't help but wonder why we needed the
Negro...why we needed a Master.
To live in shadows like that for most of our lives
...we both feel a sense of disgrace...shame...
The difficult position we find ourselves now
in the eyes of the world...I am sure this makes you
very unhappy...anxious...even disquieted, perhaps.

DIFFERENT YET THE SAME
by Maddie

A simple lesson
Of love that's limitless
Just by letting me feel you
And allowing all of me to be felt,

Helping me understand
That we are individual extensions
Of the same
Unrelated packages
Carrying a unified message.

At times we fail to recognize
That while our outside may be diverse
We all bleed red,
Different yet the same.

You live, you fall,
You fail and hope you have learned,
Sometimes taking a while
To comprehend.

We hate, we love
In our own way
Like carbon copies
Of a rare blend,
Different yet the same,

Analyzing joy and pain,
Interpreting feelings,
Careful, detailed, without mistakes
We see ourselves in one another and understand

Regardless of how our exterior is made
We are Unique, single individuals,

On the outside different,
Yet inside
Our makeup is the same!

CALLING ALL PEOPLE
by C.J.

This is a call to arms,
to my brothers and sisters of Earth,
to collectively bond together,
to see differences not as defective,
but as unique tools of strength,
to denounce the size of a person's wallet
equaling the scope of their opportunity,
to elevate character, heart, and drive
as determiners of our fate
to affect the world around us.
This is a call to action.

Violence creates nothing but a momentary reaction.
Rage must be reigned in for true metamorphosis to
        begin.
Obsolete here are guns and fists. Brains have better
        uses.
Make marks on the world that last longer than
        fading bruises.
Overcome the fear and anger, which consume and
        smother.
Instead of breaking glass, shatter the mindsets of

others.
Use emotions to focus with purpose before using
      your mouth
to effect actions leading a path out of this steep
      spiral south.

Renounce being silent; use your strong voice.
Let passive activism be your choice.
With passions of many, transition evolves.
To set it in motion, all must get involved.

Stroke no mere checks, in hopes of tax deductions.
With both feet, leap to the heart of production;
at communal gardens, shelters, food banks,
schools, hospitals; join the volunteer ranks.
Create lasting bonds with community neighbors;
commit to parting friends, though meeting as
      strangers.
Instead of just clicking a button and creating a list,
walk among the people. Clear your head of
      isolation's mist.

Lead by example and set precedence.
Demonstrate substance in lieu of decadence.
Let your fingers around an ink pen close,
declare outrage, expressing bardic prose.
Plaster revolutionary notes for all to see.
Use your gifts and talents for something bigger
      than thee.
Compose protest songs, publish them, and sing

them freely,
Organize the masses. Demand better by decree.
Resistance should be visible, leading others to
        discuss;
forget asking what's in it for you, ask what's in it for
        us.

Refuse to be a spectator. Resist being dictated, too.
Accept absolutely nothing and no one at face value.
Take a firm, two handed grasp on your reality,
actively creating bright future totality.
Spit out the corrupt system's spoon fed knowledge.
Question; true learning extends beyond college.
Have what you stand for in your conscience align.
Turn off the TV and make a picket sign.
Write a letter to your congressmen.
Visit their office. Stage a sit in.
Link your arms together in a chain when
forces come to evict with aggression
from grassy squares, parks, and legislative steps.
Rise together, chant unity with each breath.

This is a call to arms
to my brothers and sisters of Earth
to collectively bond together,
to see differences not as defective
but as unique tools of strength,
to denounce the size of a person's wallet
equaling the scope of their opportunity,
to elevate character, heart, and drive

as determiners of our fate,
to affect the world around us.
This is a call to action.

I CANNOT LEAVE YOU OUT OF THIS SACRED CIRCLE OF HUMANITY
by Betty

Why does slavery continue to stalk our
      unconscious,
continue to look into the windows of our parked
      cars
as if to reveal our deepest injury?
That somehow driving our bodies like cars reveals a
      lost world,
an answer to this question—How does it feel to be
      the problem?

It has gone on long enough, more than 500 years.
So it's time we know that we bathe in the same
      ocean
and there is always, always
this backdrop of beauty, and infinite space.
Our bodies cannot be left out of this question,
This sacred circle of humanity.

THE END